ORGANIZATIONAL VISION, VALUES AND MISSION

Cynthia D. Scott, M.P.H., Ph.D.
Dennis T. Jaffe, Ph.D.
Glenn R. Tobe, M.A.

A FIFTY-MINUTE™ SERIES BOOK

CRISP PUBLICATIONS, INC.
Menlo Park, California

ORGANIZATIONAL VISION, VALUES AND MISSION

Cynthia D. Scott, M.P.H., Ph.D.
Dennis T. Jaffe, Ph.D.
Glenn R. Tobe, M.A.

CREDITS:
Editor: **Kay Kepler**
Typesetting: **ExecuStaff**
Cover Design: **Carol Harris**
Artwork: **Ralph Mapson**

Copyright © 1993 Crisp Publications, Inc.
Printed in the United States of America by Bawden Printing Company.

English language Crisp books are distributed worldwide. Our major international distributors include:

CANADA: Reid Publishing Ltd., Box 69559—109 Thomas St., Oakville, Ontario, Canada L6J 7R4. TEL: (905) 842-4428, FAX: (905) 842-9327

Raincoast Books Distribution Ltd., 112 East 3rd Avenue, Vancouver, British Columbia, Canada V5T 1C8. TEL: (604) 873-6581, FAX: (604) 874-2711

AUSTRALIA: Career Builders, P.O. Box 1051, Springwood, Brisbane, Queensland, Australia 4127. TEL: 841-1061, FAX: 841-1580

NEW ZEALAND: Career Builders, P.O. Box 571, Manurewa, Auckland, New Zealand. TEL: 266-5276, FAX: 266-4152

JAPAN: Phoenix Associates Co., Mizuho Bldg. 2-12-2, Kami Osaki, Shinagawa-Ku, Tokyo 141, Japan. TEL: 3-443-7231, FAX: 3-443-7640

Selected Crisp titles are also available in other languages. Contact International Rights Manager Suzanne Kelly at (415) 323-6100 for more information.

Library of Congress Catalog Card Number 92-70921
Scott, Cynthia, Dennis Jaffe, and Glenn Tobe
Organizational Vision, Values and Mission
ISBN 1-56052-210-0

This book is printed on recyclable paper with soy ink.

ABOUT THIS BOOK

Organizational Vision, Values and Mission is not like most books. It has a unique "self-study" format that encourages a reader to become personally involved. Designed to be "read with a pencil," there is an abundance of exercises, activities, assessments and cases that invite participation.

The purpose of this book is to give the reader an understanding of the process of visioning and the importance of individual, group and organizational values. This book will show how these elements fit together to create a coherent, aligned and productive organization.

Organizational Vision, Values and Mission (and the other self-improvement books listed in the back of this book) can be used effectively in a number of ways. Here are some possibilities:

—**Individual Study.** Because the book is self-instructional, all that is needed is a quiet place, some time and a pencil. By completing the activities and exercises, a reader should not only receive valuable feedback, but also practical steps in creating a more productive organization.

—**Workshops and Seminars.** The book is ideal for reading prior to a workshop or seminar. With the basics in hand, the quality of participation will improve. More time can be spent on concept extensions and applications during the program. The book is also effective when a trainer distributes it at the beginning of a session and leads participants through the contents.

—**Remote Location Training.** Copies can be sent to those not able to attend "home office" training sessions.

—**Informal Study Groups.** Thanks to the format, brevity and low cost, this book is ideal for "brown-bag" or other information group sessions.

There are other possibilities that depend on the objectives, program or ideas of the user. One thing is certain; even after it has been read, this book will serve as excellent reference material that can be easily reviewed.

ABOUT THE AUTHORS

Cynthia D. Scott, M.P.H., Ph.D.

Dr. Scott is a founding partner of HeartWork Inc. She is a recognized leader in the fields of high performance, managing organizational change and visionary leadership.

She earned her M.P.H. in health planning at the University of Michigan and her Ph.D. in clinical psychology at The Fielding Institute. She is a licensed clinical psychologist.

Dr. Scott is the author of several books, including *Take This Job and Love It, StressMap, Empowerment, and Managing Organization Change.*

Dennis T. Jaffe, Ph.D.

Dr. Jaffe is a founding partner of HeartWork Inc. He is nationally recognized in the fields of executive team development, visionary leadership and new models of health care. He consults with organizations on managing organizational change, long-range planning and designing collaborative workplaces.

He earned an M.A. in management and a Ph.D. in sociology at Yale. Dr. Jaffe is a professor at Saybrook Institute, where he serves as director of doctoral studies in organizational inquiry. Dr. Jaffe is a licensed clinical psychologist.

Dr. Jaffe is the author of numerous books, including *Healing from Within, Take This Job and Love It, Working with the Ones You Love,* and *Managing Organizational Change.* Two of his books received the *Medical Self-Care Book Award.*

Dr. Scott and Dr. Jaffe are co-designers of training and assessment tools, including *StressMap and Activating Empowerment.* Their video, *Managing People Through Change,* was selected as one of the best of 1990 by *Human Resource Executive.*

Glenn R. Tobe, M.A.

Glenn Tobe is a principal of HeartWork Inc. His work is mobilizing organizations to provide outstanding customer service while developing a competitive advance. He has been actively involved in the Malcolm Baldridge award as a means of creating organizational excellence.

Mr. Tobe is a member of the faculty at San Francisco State University. He earned his B.A. in Business Administration from Columbia Pacific University and his M.A. in clinical psychology from John F. Kennedy University.

Mr. Tobe has written numerous articles on building high- performance teams and leadership development, and has been featured in the *San Francisco Chronicle*, the *Contra Costa Times*, and the *San Jose Mercury News*.

Mr. Tobe is a well-known speaker, consultant and keynote speaker. His recent clients include Pacific Gas and Electric, IBM, Pacific Bell, Kaiser Permanente, and Delta Dental.

HeartWork, Inc. is a consulting firm whose mission is to create high-performance workplaces by aligning individuals, teams and the whole organization around values, vision and a clear mission, and empowering everyone to become part of this process and take action to make it a reality. This book is based on HeartWork's **Vision Retreats,** which have helped scores of teams and organizations get back on track by discovering and clarifying their essences. HeartWork has affiliates all over the country.

For more information on keynotes, retreats and implementing major strategic decisions, please call:

HeartWork, Inc.
461 Second Street, Suite 232
San Francisco, CA 94107-1416
(415) 546-4488

CONTENTS

INTRODUCTION

The present is a time of upheaval and change in organizations. Companies are challenging the ways they do business. They need to innovate, adapt, shift and transform themselves. For an organization to succeed today, every employee needs to exhibit leadership, make decisions and act on opportunities. But with all this change, what are the keys that help to keep a person and an organization on track?

Visioning includes the processes of clarifying values, focusing mission and stretching to a preferred vision. These key elements form the essence around which individuals, teams and organizations plot their course.

Some of these questions that will be answered by this book are:

- How do I know how to act if things continually change?

- How do I embody my organization's values and make decisions using these values?

- How can the organization create a unified purpose with so many different values?

- How can an organization involve people in the creation of a shared vision?

In this book you'll have an opportunity to clarify your own values in the context of work, revisit the mission of your group and organization and create a compelling vision statement for your work group. You'll look at ways to communicate and implement strategies for reaching this goal. This book is about what it takes to clarify and sustain visions as a force for high performance.

The Process
of Visioning

UNDERSTANDING THE PROCESS

"The best way to predict the future is to invent it"
—Alan Kay, scientist, inventor

Visioning is a journey from the known to the unknown, which helps create the future from a montage of facts, hopes, dreams, dangers and opportunities.

One of the key characteristics of high-performance organizations and teams is that they have a clear picture of what they are trying to create together, they are excited and clear about their basic purpose and they share a common set of values. The values, mission and vision form the core of their identity. These key elements constitute the glue that keeps people, teams and organizations responsive and innovative in new situations.

Visioning refers to the process of clarifying values, focusing a mission and stretching the horizon with a vision. It is not a one-time meeting that a group engages in and then forgets. Visioning has stages that can be accomplished over time. Visioning evokes creative solutions to business challenges and sparks continual evolution and learning in an organization.

ELEMENTS OF THE VISIONING PROCESS

When engaging in the visioning process, it is important to include all the following elements in the process.

1. *Values* are the principles, the standards, the actions that people in an organization represent, which they consider inherently worthwhile and of the utmost importance. They include: how people treat each other, how people, groups and organizations conduct their business and about what is most important to the organization.

2. *Scanning* the current situation involves looking beyond the organization to its customers and suppliers and industry trends for information on what is important to them. Involving the internal customers—the employees—is also an important part of the process.

3. *Mission* is the core purpose for which a person, team or organization is created. It is summarized in a clear, short, inspiring statement that focuses attention in one clear direction by stating the purpose of the individual's, business's or group's uniqueness.

4. *Visioning* is picturing excellence—what the person, team or organization wants to create in its best possible future. It is an evocative description of what is possible. A vision is not ''something out there'' that is impractical, but a way of setting a compelling scenario. Creating this image of the future requires the ability to expand one's sense of possibilities and then focus on what new initiatives can lead to success.

5. *Implementation* includes the strategy, plans, procedures and key actions that will put all of the above into action.

Five-Step Visioning Sequence

| STEP 1: | **Clarify Values**
Define key values and what they mean in action |

STEP 1: **Clarify Values**
Define key values and what they mean in action

STEP 2: **Scan the Current Situation**
Examine the current environment internally and externally

STEP 3: **Define the Mission**
Clarify the basic purpose

STEP 4: **Create a Vision**
Generate a clear image of the preferred future

STEP 5: **Implement the Vision**
Create strategic plans, action plans and feedback loops to implement the values, vision and mission.

THE ESSENCE-DRIVEN ORGANIZATION

Studies have shown that visioning, planning and goal-setting can improve organizational performance. Attractive visions of the future have great power. We call the organization that is organized around a deep sense of values, mission and vision the essence-driven organization. This kind of organization has tapped the energy that results from its own clarity of direction and focus. The essence-driven organization has a greater capacity to weather changes in marketplace and customer demand because of the clarity of its core purpose. An organization driven by its essence knows its purpose and why it is important. Organizations that are tied to their essence are more powerful, command more commitment from employees and can get more done in a changing environment.

Why Do Organizations Vision?

- Brings people together around a common dream
- Coordinates the work of different people
- Helps everyone make decisions
- Builds foundation for business planning
- Challenges the comfortable or inadequate present state
- Makes incongruent behavior more noticeable

Problem Solving Versus Visioning

Visioning is different from problem solving. Problem solving is about incremental improvements. Visioning lays the foundation for breakthrough improvements by allowing the mind to break free of its assumptions about how things are done and looking differently at what can be done and how. It invites you to look at the organization in new ways.

ORGANIZATIONAL RENEWAL CYCLE

Organizations go through cycles as part of their growth and development. Organizations and groups choose different times to revisit and revise their inner identity. Most organizations start out with a clear purpose and a lot of energy. Organizations or teams in this early phase are having fun and growing their dream. They have a compelling vision, and they are propelled to make it happen.

After its initial period of creative excitement, the organization or group enters stability or managed growth. They build structure to ensure that their purpose is carried out consistently and define the way things are done. But in doing so, they inevitably lose something. Organizations at this developmental stage predictably become set in their ways and lose their ability to innovate and respond to the market place. Eventually, company employees feel that the magic has gone out of the work and now it's "just" work. Sometimes a shift in the environment, maturing of a product or a crisis pressures the organization or group to act differently. It needs to change.

An opportunity to begin a new phase begins with the realization that the initial energy can be recaptured. The visioning process offers the company an opportunity to change and become more vital. Visioning allows the organization to take a hard look at itself. What does it do, who are its customers, what basic assumptions does it operate from and what internal processes reinforce its values? Visioning revisits the values and mission and engages the organization in seeing new possibilities.

ORGANIZATIONAL RENEWAL CYCLE (continued)

Individual Renewal Cycle

People as well as organizations go through cycles of renewal. Using this model to look at your own career, think back and identify what happened to you in each of these phases.

Phase 1—Creativity

_____

_____

Phase 2—Stability

_____

_____

Phase 3—Renewal

_____

_____

Organizational Renewal Cycle

Now focus on your team or organization. What period are you in right now? What could move you into being ready for renewal?

Phase 1—Creativity

_____

_____

Phase 2—Stability

_____

_____

Phase 3—Renewal

_____

_____

The Organizational Renewal Cycle

Phase 1. Creativity

▶ Work is on purpose

▶ Excitement about finding a new ideal model/product/market

▶ Lots of vision

▶ Chaotic/fun atmosphere

▶ Growth is fast and easy, almost natural

Phase 2. Stability

▶ Purpose stays the same

▶ Structure solidifies with policies, procedures, standards

▶ Controls set in, standards are enforced

▶ Management becomes more ''professional''

▶ Thinking about the future and planning is done at the top

Crisis
- The environment changes
- Standards are enforced from the top
- People work harder
- Results slip
- Group runs out of steam, loses vitality

Phase 3. Renewal

▶ Revisit basic purpose

▶ Renew mission, values and vision

▶ Redefine, question what the organization is doing

▶ Reconnect with customers/market

▶ Forge new directions

VISIONARY LEADERSHIP

During a period of organizational renewal, the manager becomes central to the visioning process. The manager often leads this process, during which people and teams clarify their values, visit their mission and create exciting visions.

The role of the manager is to articulate and define what has been implied or unsaid in the organization. The visioning process uses different steps to provide a focus for attention. People want a sense of direction and meaning to pull together organizational actions. Using images, metaphors and models helps the people in the team or organization understand what is going on.

For the manager, the process of leading visioning is far different from the more traditional planning, controlling and scheduling. Managers who engage in visioning must be able to take the basic focus of the organization and pull it forward into the future in a way that is compelling to others.

Start Anywhere—Person, Team or Organization

As we demonstrate how to generate values, mission and vision, we will assume that this process will take place with you personally, as a team or group, and for the whole organization.

If the organization already has a vision, mission or set of values, that does not mean that you and your team have nothing to do. The task of your group is to determine how your group vision complements the vision of the organization. Individuals face the same hurdles. As each person clarifies personal values, mission and vision, the challenge becomes how to find the alignment between the personal and the organizational.

As organizations go through the process of renewal, it is possible that change will occur in the team or group first. This growth often challenges other groups to set out on the path to renewing their essence. You can start at any level of the organization—the process of clarifying essence will spread to other levels. In most cases this renewal begins with the strategic leadership of the organization in order to re-energize competitive advantage.

Creating Alignment

Alignment between the group values, mission and vision and those of the individual creates the power of a group committed to a common vision. If these values are not aligned, sooner or later, the people experience tension and frustration. Alignment means that the people in the group create their own vision that fits within the mission and vision of their organization, that defines clearly their own part in creating excellence. There needs to be one overarching vision for the entire organization and then each group creates its own vision that nests within the larger vision.

Because organizations consist of teams and groups, an important step in the visioning process is to have all the groups involved develop a shared vision, which is sometimes called nesting the visions or getting the visions aligned. This process involves steering the individual vision in the same direction as the team and organizational visions.

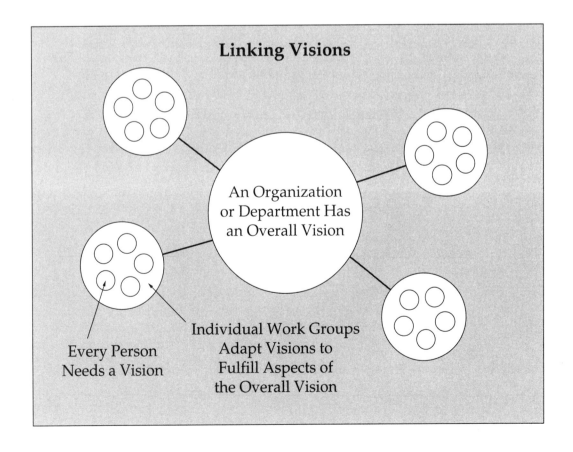

VISIONARY LEADERSHIP (continued)

How Visioning Fits into the Planning Sequence

The processes of clarifying values, revitalizing the mission and creating a vision are key to this strategic planning process. Visioning doesn't substitute for strategic and tactical plans, it is a process that comes before the plans. Organizations move from visioning to strategic planning, to yearly plans and measurements.

1. Visioning Is Emotional

When groups engage in visioning, emotions will come into play. Visioning often unleashes conflicting forces. People feel at once hope and motivation, as well as fear and anxiety about making changes. It is important to understand that if this process is not experienced emotionally, then the ''buy in'' and commitment are drastically reduced.

Groups tend to become upset and dissatisfied with the current state of functioning after they have visioned a positive alternative. If the group moves too slowly toward the vision, people become impatient and frustrated. This impatience can be channeled into a positive reaction by helping people understand that this tension is normal and predictable.

2. Visioning Is an Organizational Change Process

Shared visions are the foundation for making change. Without shared vision, new ways of thinking or acting are inhibited by the pull of how things have been in the past. But without real change, visioning is pointless and counter-productive. Starting a visioning process without understanding that it is a part of a larger organizational change process is to undertake a hazardous enterprise. Clarifying values, mission and vision often calls into question basic assumptions about work design, direction, leadership and strategy. The process of conducting an organizational scan, clarifying mission and vision can mean that people in the organization become more empowered and committed to the results.

3. *Visioning Requires Involvement*

One of the most important parts of this whole process is the amount of involvement of the key stakeholders. It is tempting to take a small "representative" group off to do the visioning and then deliver the mission and vision to everyone else. This method may seem like a prudent use of time for the organization, but people will not be committed to the discoveries of others, and much effort will be wasted. It pays to spend more time in the planning and gathering and discussing of the analysis, mission and vision, because the buy-in will be substantially stronger and the implementation phase will just be a continuation of the process, rather than a disjointed hand-off from planners to doers. Involvement needs to be widespread.

The core of this process is a design team that spans all levels of the organization and represents all important stakeholder groups. This group needs to be carefully selected and given the necessary amount of release time and resources to accomplish the task. These teams are the most successful when participation in this process is part of their job description and performance review.

Always keep the larger organization apprised of what the team is doing. Communication of the overall process in newsletters, meetings and other methods is very important. At some point, everyone in the organization should feel that they have input into the process. Those who craft the process, own it.

Visioning Hits the Wall

Many visioning projects have fallen flat because they questioned basic assumptions of the organization and fundamental structural relationships. Often organizations wanted to have a vision but didn't want to learn or respond to what they found out. At this point, some efforts reach an impasse. To ensure that people do not become disillusioned, it is important to think the process all the way through and make sure that leadership will support the changes necessary for reaching the vision.

VISIONARY LEADERSHIP (continued)

Principles of Visioning

- If people create the vision, they will own it and the implementation of the vision will happen more quickly

- The process of developing the vision is as important as its outcome

- Visions are best stated in the language of the key stakeholders

- Vision helps to focus the strategic planning process and therefore needs to be developed before planning takes place

Example of Organizational Visioning

It is helpful to see an example of visioning process to get a sense of the steps involved and the time that it can take to go through the process completely. This list is used to ensure that all the aspects are covered.

1. Create a representative design team for the organization that guides the visioning process.

2. Design team scans environment and drafts a statement that summarizes why the organization exists, what businesses it is in, what products and services, customers and what value you bring to them.

3. Design team compares their statement to any existing mission statements.

4. Design team generates questions they think the vision statement should answer.

5. Visioning tools get people thinking creatively about the vision questions.

6. Design team drafts a mission and vision statement.

7. Circulate the draft statements to key decision makers and members of the organization. Incorporate their feedback.

8. Communicate the mission and vision to your organization, groups with which you interact and your customers.

Checklist for Organizing the Visioning Process

1. This process is being applied to (circle one):

    My total organization

    A function of the organization (which one?)

    Major division

    Team

    Myself

2. Identify three critical issues you hope this visioning process will address.

    1. _____

    2. _____

    3. _____

3. List three major obstacles to visioning.

    1. _____

    2. _____

    3. _____

1

Clarify Values

IDENTIFYING VALUES

"We've learned . . . that the soft stuff and the hard stuff are becoming increasingly intertwined. A company's values—what it stands for, what its people believe in—are crucial to its competitive success. Indeed, values drive the business."

—Robert Haas, Chairman and CEO, Levi Strauss

A person's values answer the question "What's important to me?" Our values are the deepseated pervasive standards that influence almost every aspect of our lives: our moral judgments, our responses to others, our commitments to personal and organizational goals. We all have belief systems we live by. Our beliefs and value systems are deeply connected. We are motivated and make decisions based on these belief systems and values. Often these values are unconscious.

If we all had the same values with the same priorities, it would be easy to work in groups. Most teams, however, have a diversity of values and beliefs. To help us work better as a team and make decisions that lead to commitment and action, it is necessary to see the range of values that influence the decision-making process and find ways to prioritize and clarify the values used.

Definition

Values are defined by Webster's dictionary as "a principle standard or quality considered inherently worthwhile or desirable." The root for value is *valor*, which means strength. Values are sources of strength, because they give people the power to take action. Values are deep and emotional and often difficult to change.

Values are the Foundation for Vision

Values are the essence of a company's philosophy for achieving success. They are the bedrock of corporate culture. Values provide employees with a sense of common direction and guidelines for day-to-day behavior.

IDENTIFYING VALUES (continued)

Meaning at Work

The first step in creating an atmosphere of common commitment is to invite the hearts and minds of employees to join the purpose of the company. One of the vital things people look for in their work is the meaning of what they are doing. People need to feel that what they do goes beyond the immediate activities to affect others in a positive and profound way. You need to see the connection between your actions and a greater purpose. For example, many people have stuffed envelopes to further an initiative they support. Stuffing the envelopes may have been rather boring, but the reason sustained them.

What is the meaning of the work that you do?

_____

_____

_____

_____

_____

_____

_____

_____

_____

_____

_____

_____

Shared mission, values and vision brings people together. They unite and provide the link between diverse people and activities. A shared essence is the expression of what people have in common, of what they, in community, are committed to. People who share values or vision are more likely to take responsibility; they are more likely to challenge the bounds of convention. In organizations where this essence is developed, people do not assume they are powerless. They believe they have the power to contribute directly.

Values at Work

Central to a company getting the job done today is its clarity about its values. Before mission, vision and strategy, a company or group must come to agreement about what it stands for, both in its customer service and community relations, and within itself, in its dealings with employees. As employees face increasing responsibility, making more complex and far-reaching decisions, a corporate values credo is an essential standard for behavior. How you achieve your goals and vision is as important as the goal itself.

Groups have become concerned with defining their vision of the future and their mission, a statement about their purpose. The vision and mission are incomplete in that they define only the major external focus. Clarity about values provides the underlying foundation for action.

In addition to its mission and vision, a group must also determine how they will work together, how they will treat each other and what bonds them together. People work for different reasons and want different things from each other and the organization. It is possible that a group agrees on a vision and mission, but lapses into conflict because different people have different values about working together. Some members might want to work on their own, some want lots of interaction, while others see the workplace as an arena for personal competition and "winning" through good results. Team and individual values exploration will make these differences explicit and lead to the building of a team values statement.

LINKING PERSONAL AND ORGANIZATIONAL VALUES

If employees know what their company stands for, if they know what standards they are to uphold, then they are much more likely to make decisions that will support those standards. They are also more likely to feel as if they are an important part of the organization. They are motivated because life in the company has meaning for them.

—Terrence E. Deal and Allan A. Kennedy, Corporate Cultures

One of the most important keys to greater effectiveness is a close link between personal and organizational values. A survey by the American Management Association of 1,460 managers and chief executives suggests that an understanding of this relationship will provide new leverage for corporate vitality. This relationship, when mismanaged, can provide the breeding ground for conflict and cynicism. The survey provided solid evidence that shared values between the individual and the company are a major source of both personal and organizational effectiveness.

The same report showed that when managers' values were congruent with the values of their companies, their personal lives were in better shape, their approach to their job more optimistic and their stress lower. Employees' sense of what is important strongly influences their commitment and motivation.

Values Provide Guidance

Values are one of our most special achievements as human beings. A person acts not just in service to personal needs, but also out of a broader sense of what is important and meaningful. In fact, values are the deepest and most powerful motivators of personal action.

Values represent an organizing principle for our lives, as well as for an organization. What is most important to us to accomplish, and to do, at work, in our family and in our personal life and career, can be described in relation to the values we want to achieve.

Sometimes we mistakenly think of values as a series of "shoulds," telling us what we can and cannot do. This approach is a very limited way to see values. Rather, values are energizing, motivating and inspiring. When we care passionately about something, when we value it, we can spur ourselves on to great achievements. The highest achievements of people and organizations arise when they feel inspired to accomplish something that fits their highest values. Values are at the root of all learning.

In our lives we have met people who live out values that are important in our own lives. Think back about the people who have made a significant difference in your life or in the lives of others. What are the values that they exemplify?

Values of people I have admired: How I can act on these values:

_____   _____

_____   _____

_____   _____

_____   _____

_____   _____

_____   _____

_____   _____

LINKING PERSONAL AND ORGANIZATIONAL VALUES (continued)

Values Replace Rules

While there will always be differences of emphasis and increasing diversity of values among employees, creating consensus about key values is an important task for any group. Employees at every level must face customers, make costly decisions and balance competing priorities.

Previously, agreement was generated by having strict procedures and standards of behavior, which were enforced by supervisors. Today, with more empowerment and a greater sphere of autonomy for individual employees, people need to be guided not by rules, or by supervisors, but by under-standing the most important values held by the organization. If a decision fits the values, then it is right.

Think back to some of the rules that have been used in your previous workplaces:

1. _____

2. _____

3. _____

4. _____

Now see which values are underlying these rules. List some of the values that can guide your actions at work:

1. _____

2. _____

3. _____

4. _____

Aligned Values

When you work in an environment where your work activities are aligned with what you consider important, your energy, motivation, desire and will to achieve even the most difficult tasks seem to emerge. Therefore, clarifying personal and work values can be a great resource for an organization. First we clarify our values for ourselves, and then for our team and organization. Sometimes our most important or most neglected values remain obscure. Unclear or unknown values can produce conflicts and contradictions that can make people feel confused, blocked and frustrated.

Undiscussed Values

Values provide the foundation for the strategy, the mission and the structure. Values are a set of understandings in an organization about how to work together, how to treat other people and what is most important. These understandings are the core values. In most organizations they are understood, but they are seldom discussed. Most organizational and team values are unconscious, in that they lie below the surface and are not openly explored or discussed. Bringing them into the light of day enhances agreement and connection.

Unconscious values in my group/team/organization

_____

_____

_____

_____

_____

_____

LINKING PERSONAL AND ORGANIZATIONAL VALUES (continued)

Change of Values

Research conducted on American values found that until recently, values have remained quite stable over time. Of the six values ranked highest in 1968 (honesty, ambition, responsibility, forgiveness, broadmindedness and courage) the same were ranked highest in 1981. The stability of the least preferred (imagination, logic, obedience, intelligence, politeness, independence) had similar stability. In this 13-year period it was also found that American society was undergoing changes in certain values, shifting away from a collective norm to a more individualized orientation.

Values are the meaning we attach to things. Our earliest values revolve around our parents and the people who take care of us. As people grow they develop other values. These revolve around things we learn about in the larger community and school. These learned values are associated with our basic growth and development. Later we develop values that are related to work, becoming independent and providing for yourself. Later on some people develop values related to the human community in general.

More recently, the values of teamwork, independence and creativity have moved onto the lists of most important values. This signals some major value shifts in what people want from the workplace and how people want their organizations to be designed. They want more participation and creative involvement in defining not just what they do, but what the organization is all about—its essence.

Values Into Action

People assume certain basic values, rarely questioning them. People act from their values, and different people value different things. In fact, values are motivators, since when we feel that something is right and important we will spend a great deal of effort to achieve it. To be effective, a company needs some agreement about what it values. It has to turn these values, in turn, into policies, practices and standards for behavior. A company's or group's values thus focus the behavior of people in all of their activities.

Questions for a Group to Clarify Values

- What do we stand for? _____
  _____

- What behaviors would mirror these values? _____
  _____

- How do we treat our employees? _____
  _____

- How do we treat our customers? _____
  _____

- What do we mean by ethical behavior? _____
  _____

- What are the core values that are more important to us than profits?
  _____
  _____

- How do we want to treat each other at work? _____
  _____

- What do we offer our employees for their work effort? _____
  _____

- How do we want to be seen by the community? _____
  _____

- What attitudes and behavior in employees do we want to reward?
  _____
  _____

LINKING PERSONAL AND ORGANIZATIONAL VALUES (continued)

Value Conflicts

Sometimes values are espoused or acted upon that contradict or conflict with other values. These are values conflicts. What if a company values honesty, but also values a high sales volume? How or when does the value of honesty supersede the value of making a sale? Many companies have been deeply wounded by such value conflicts, most often because employees did not feel they had a forum to explore or discuss these conflicts. A values exchange and discussion is critical to clarifying the limits of behavior and personal responsibility.

For example, one company with a strong values orientation reported that they were given a huge order from a tobacco company, with the condition that they eliminate their corporate no-smoking policy. The company debated the order within every work group, balancing the need for the order with the challenge to its values. Finally, the different work groups achieved consensus that their value on health promotion was more important than the order, and they turned it down rather than change their policy.

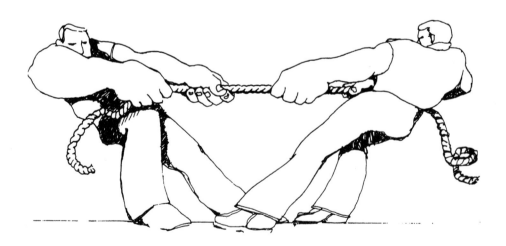

VALUES CARDS

In the back of the book are several pages that contain cards representing important values. These pages are perforated and can be detached from the book. After you detach the pages, you need to cut the values cards along the lines indicated. You will create a deck of cards, with each of the important values on one card. There are also some reference cards as well.

Personal Values Exploration

Use the HeartWork Values Cards© for personal self-exploration or as a tool for building a work team. Clarifying values for a team and organization is an essential activity within an organization. When people know why they are there, a shared commitment grows.

Like all tools, the cards do nothing by themselves, but rather help you to clarify your thoughts. The values cards evolved as a tool for helping people clarify their values. In the beginning when we asked people about their key values, we found that some people had difficulty coming up with a comprehensive list. So, after years of sorting, we brought together the most commonly expressed values on cards to help people focus on what is important to them.

VALUES CARDS AHEAD . . .

VALUES CARDS (continued)

Using the Values Cards

There are 50 cards, each one representing a particular value. Each value has an icon, like the suit from a deck of cards, that indicates a value category. Five additional "column heading" cards are labeled as follows:

> **Always Valued**
>
> **Often Valued**
>
> **Sometimes Valued**
>
> **Seldom Valued**
>
> **Least Valued**

Some cards are labeled "wild card." If you have an important value that is not represented in the deck, you can add your own value by writing it in on the wild card.

ARRANGING YOUR VALUES CARDS

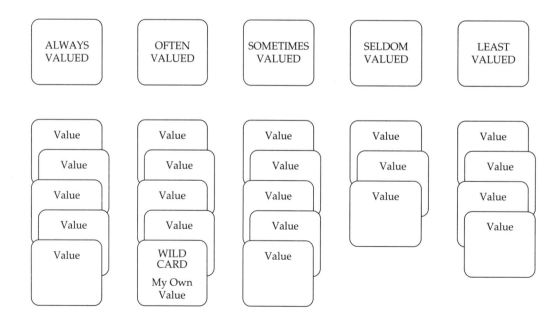

Sorting Your Values

Begin your personal values exploration by placing the five column heading cards across the top of a table in the order listed. They form the top of five columns. Place each value card in the column that indicates how central or important that value is in your life. Sort the cards so there are 10 in each column. It will take some time, and you will probably end up moving your cards back and forth between columns. See the arrangement diagram on the previous page for a picture of how the sorted values columns will possibly look.

At first you may feel that all the values are important to you, and you will want to put most of them under the "Always" or "Often" valued columns. But remember, the purpose of the values sort is to indicate your values in order of their importance to you at this time in your life. Some will be less important values because you have to set priorities in your life. When sorting your values, try to think of specific examples of how that value applies to your life. If you can't think of a specific example, it probably is not your highest priority value.

After you have sorted the cards into the columns, try to arrange the cards in each column from most important to least important. Put the most important cards at the top of the column, down to the least important. In that way, you will ultimately have sorted all 50 values from most to least important. This exercise will help you determine which are the central values guiding your life.

VALUES CARDS (continued)

My Top-Five Values:

1. _____

2. _____

3. _____

4. _____

5. _____

Values Into Action

After writing down each value, write a specific example of how you express that value in your work (or in your life).

1. _____
   _____

2. _____
   _____

3. _____
   _____

4. _____
   _____

5. _____
   _____

Additional Questions

You can sort the values cards in several ways. Instead of just asking for your most important values, you can sort the cards in answer to other questions. For example, you might ask:

- Which values have you not focused on, or neglected, in your life?

  _____

  _____

- Which values are most important to you in your work?

  _____

  _____

- Which values are most important to your personal or family life?

  _____

  _____

- Which values receive the most attention in your workplace?

  _____

  _____

VALUES AND TEAMS

The values cards are a tool for clarifying individual and team values. Values don't mean much if you keep them secret. If you are willing to share and express your values to the people around you, you are more likely to actualize them. It is important for people who work together to share their personal values and to clarify together what values are central to their shared work.

After each person has individually sorted his or her values, it is time to share them with the team. Have each team member place his name tag at the top of the values sort and have the group stand up and move around the room to see what values each of the other members have chosen. This is done in silence, without comment. After everyone has looked at everyone else's, then ask each person to choose the person they are *most* alike and have a shared conversation about their values. After this discussion, then have a discussion with the person they are *least* alike. After this conversation, group members usually have a deeper appreciation for individual values choice.

What are some of the similarities in your group? _____

_____

_____

_____

_____

_____

What are some of the differences? _____

_____

_____

_____

_____

_____

CREATING A TEAM VALUES CREDO

1. Selecting Your Key Values

After everyone has sorted their individual values, it's now time to work on discovering team values. Look back again at all the values and select five values that you want expressed in the workplace. Remember, not all the values that you value personally are appropriate for the workplace. Select those that you are willing to live by in the workplace.

Values I Want to Have Expressed in the Workplace.

_____

_____

_____

_____

_____

2. Sharing the Key Values

Go around the room. Each person, in turn, reads off the most important value. Have a recorder write each value on a flip chart. When it is your turn, if your value is already up on the flip chart, the recorder places a check after it. When everyone has named their most important value, begin a second round. Continue until five rounds of voting have taken place. Now you will have a record of the key values of the group. The number of check marks after each indicate how many people considered this a key value.

Key Values for This Group

_____

_____

_____

_____

_____

CREATING A TEAM VALUES CREDO
(continued)

3. Ranking Key Team Values

Arrange the values in a list, from the one with the most check marks, to the ones that have the least check marks. These are a listing of the team's key values. It is best to come up with a limited number of core values; five to seven seems to work best for focusing a group. You might also look at some of the important values, and cluster together those that are similar to each other. You might take one of the value names for that cluster, or give some of the cluster names that combine the meanings of the values within them.

Our Key Values Ranked in Order of Importance

#1. _____

#2. _____

#3. _____

#4. _____

#5. _____

4. Discuss Gaps

The team now can use its list of key values as a foundation for a discussion. Discuss for each key value some of the ways that people express that value in their work. Ask yourselves:

Which of the values are not expressed frequently enough? _____

_____

Which values tend to be forgotten? _____

_____

Which values are neglected in times of pressure? _____

_____

Which values sometimes seem dispensable? _____

_____

5. Neglected or Unexpressed Values

Often a team has certain values that they feel are espoused, but not really enacted. Members might select values the team needs to develop, or values that are expressed but neglected. Then people can select ways they can practice that value in their group.

Values the Team Needs to Develop

_____

_____

_____

_____

_____

_____

6. Create a Group Credo

The creation of an organizational values statement can be a powerful influence to align everyone to the core principles behind the organization. A values credo is not a mission statement. It expresses the values that are important.

Our Group Credo

_____

_____

_____

_____

_____

_____

CREATING A TEAM VALUES CREDO (continued)

7. **Linking Behaviors to Values**

These questions will help the team explore to what degree individuals live their values and which values are espoused, but may be neglected or even ignored. You might also discuss behaviors of a team member that reflect that value. In this way the essence and implications of each value become clear.

1. _____ *(Team Value)*

Behaviors that would show support of this value. _____

_____

2. _____ *(Team Value)*

Behaviors that would show support of this value. _____

_____

3. _____ *(Team Value)*

Behaviors that would show support of this value. _____

_____

4. _____ *(Team Value)*

Behaviors that would show support of this value. _____

_____

5. _____ *(Team Value)*

Behaviors that would show support of this value. _____

_____

EXAMPLES OF TEAM VALUE STATEMENTS

In working with a faculty group in a University of California medical center, the group evolved the following statement to represent the underlying values on which they designed their training program for nurse practitioners and physician assistants.

- The means are not separate from the ends in the practice of health care

- Self-care, self-awareness and self-referenced behavior are essential practices for educators in order to teach these skills to our students

- Relationships with our patients are focused on assisting them to return to a state of physical, mental and emotional well-being

- The real art of health care is based on the humanistic application of scientific knowledge

- A desire to re-emphasize the importance of attitudinal, interpersonal and self-care issues is necessary in the education of health professionals

- The task of educators is to provide the best possible technical training along with the transmission and articulation of ideas and values

Another example comes from Frank Nahser, who runs an advertising agency in Chicago that bears his name. He has placed his value statement and his mission on his business card. These values were first developed within the organization a decade ago and were recently revised on the occasion of the company's fiftieth anniversary. It reads as follows:

Our purpose is to create and implement outstanding ideas to help our clients' businesses grow, benefit the user and contribute to the well-being of society. To provide this vital service, our experience has led us to believe in the importance of certain values—the characteristics of deeply committed people working in a supportive community.

Organizational Values: *growth, fairness, responsibility, respect and our* ***Personal Values:*** *integrity, hard work, talent*

Organizational Vision, Values and Mission

EXAMPLES OF TEAM VALUE STATEMENTS (continued)

If you were printing up a card with your values, what would you put down?

Organizational Values

_____

_____

_____

_____

Personal Values

_____

_____

_____

_____

Values Through the Life Cycle

As you grow, different values take on importance and others seem to fade. This happens because the environment you live and work in is changing and your values adapt to it.

Look back over the last five years of your life and see which values have grown more important. Which have grown less important?

More Important

_____

_____

Less Important

_____

_____

VALUE CLUSTERS

Values mean different things to different people. Some values represent ideals that we experience as just good in themselves. These are end values, or what have been termed intrinsic values. Other values pertain to how one should do things, the style of action and relationships to others. These are called instrumental values. The following model represents one way that we have found useful to classify different types of values.

Look back over your values and notice the symbol on each card. Each one represents a cluster of values. Different values categories appear on different cards marked with different icons representing a specific category. Each area represents a different direction, or preference set. The main categories are:

1. **Social Responsibility** ▲

2. **Mastery** ✠

3. **Self Development** ♥

4. **Relationship** ☎

5. **Continuity** ✚

6. **Lifestyle** ✹

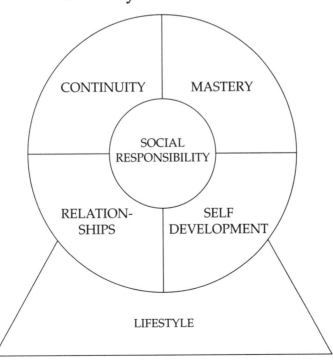

VALUE CLUSTERS (continued)

The center of the model includes social responsibility, the values that are central to maintaining civilization. Clustered around this group are four areas: mastery, self-development, relationships and continuity. These represent four directions in which a person develops values about work. Each cluster is an important area of development, none more important than another. On the bottom is the lifestyle cluster—the choices related to how one lives. Choices tend to have more or less importance based on where one is in the life cycle.

Cluster I: Social Responsibility

The values in this group are often considered good in themselves. There is no way to argue or prove, for example, that tolerance is more important than tradition or family. Each person simply holds one value more strongly than another.

Very few people would consider any of these values unimportant. However, since we only have a finite amount of time, life consists of making choices about how we spend our time and energy. Using the values cards will enable you to look at which of these values is most central to you. You may find that you consider some values in this category to be important, but you don't do much about them. You focus most of your energy on others.

Cluster II: Mastery

These values represent the achiever or individualistic pursuits, where success is defined in terms of mastery, status, power and position. This value cluster focuses on achievement in the external world. People motivated by these values want to have visible achievements, and they want these recognized by others. They want to be in a position of authority and to be seen as "winners" in competitive situations.

Cluster III: Self Development

These values represent the search for personal challenge, creativity and self-development. This cluster is associated with experiential learning, inner development, self-actualizing or seeking. The person with these values wants to be involved in challenging and meaningful projects that expand his or her capacities. Such people seek new experiences and personal development activities.

Cluster IV: Relationship

These values represent people whose primary motivation is developing personal relationships, helping and working with other people, feeling part of a group or team and sharing experience. People who have values in this cluster seek validation from other people and define their achievements in terms of what they have done for and with others. They seek contact, communication and community at work. They value their standing with others.

Cluster V: Continuity

This cluster refers to values that focus on maintaining stability and enduring qualities. This cluster is associated with an appreciation of tradition, knowing where things fit and how people will treat each other. A person with these values does not like surprises or things out of order.

Cluster VI: Lifestyle

This cluster holds values that are related to choice of lifestyle or preference for a certain style of activity. Many value disputes are about differences in preferences. This category has to do with values about personal style that refer to the ways that people work and live, personal appearance and the way that a person approaches the world.

2

Scan the Current Situation

EXPLORING YOUR CURRENT STATE

To raise new questions, new possibilities, to regard old problems from a new angle, requires creative imagination and marks real advance in science.

—Albert Einstein, scientist

To create a context for visioning, it is necessary to have a clear idea of the environment in which the group or organization exits. It's time to take a look at your organization and the world in which you operate. Listed below are several common areas that organizations review in creating a clear picture of their situation.

Environment and Current Situation Exploration

- Review the organization's present situation

- Review the organization's history

- Revisit the energy/essence of the founders

- Assess opportunities and threats

- Conduct an environmental scan

- Assess your strengths and weaknesses

- Identify the critical issues or choices that you face regarding the future

---

Present Situation

What is the current state of the Organization? What are the services, products or programs? What are the human resources? Financial standing? Plans for the future?

This is a time for the entire team or organizational design group to ask questions to bring their perspectives of the current situation into agreement. Often this process is like the blind men describing the elephant; the organization can look very different from different perspectives. Before informed visioning can be launched, the current situation must be clearly understood.

Present Situation Assessment

What is the current state of the organization? _____

_____

What's your track record? _____

_____

What is the organizational mission? _____

_____

What are its chief products/services/programs? _____

_____

What are the core competencies of this organization? _____

_____

What is its financial standing? _____

_____

What are the plans for the future? _____

_____

HISTORY OF THE ORGANIZATION

Understanding the history of the organization is very important to helping it chart its future. It is often helpful to have people who have been in the organization the longest make a presentation about how the organization started, its original mission and services or products. What were the significant events since then—major changes, successes, failures—and what have been the values that have persisted over time? People do not move toward the future without honoring the past.

The Organization's History

How has this organization developed over time? _____

_____

What changes in strategy? _____

_____

What changes in focus? _____

_____

What products/services? _____

_____

What customers? _____

_____

What structure? _____

_____

Changes in site/location/resources? _____

_____

FOUNDING ESSENCE

How an organization begins often gives it a deep sense of purpose. Organizations that have endured often spring from a philosophical wellspring that when tapped provides nourishment for the continued challenges organizations face. What was the reason the organization was founded? What were the founders like?

Essence of the Founders

Who were the founders? _____

_____

What were the founding myths? _____

_____

Why was this organization called into being? _____

_____

What was the spirit of the organization? _____

_____

OPPORTUNITIES AND THREATS

What are the major outside forces that will make a difference in whether or not you succeed? These typically include your customers, stakeholders, competitors and strategic alliances, and the social, political, economic and technological forces that influence your business.

This phase can involve extensive data gathering from questionnaires, public focus groups, interviews with key experts and literature searches.

Major Forces from the Outside

Opportunities	**Threats**
1. _____ >	< _____
2. _____ >	< _____
3. _____ >	< _____
4. _____ >	< _____
5. _____ >	< _____

SCAN THE ENVIRONMENT

52

ENVIRONMENTAL SCAN

From an environmental perspective, what are the demographic, social and cultural trends that will affect your mission and vision? Are there changes in political leadership, legislation or global shifts that may affect your business? What are the technological innovations and economic pressures that may affect what you do?

Environmental Scan

Demographic shifts: _____

_____

Social trends: _____

_____

Cultural trends: _____

_____

Political leadership: _____

_____

Legislation: _____

_____

Global shifts: _____

_____

Technological innovations: _____

_____

Economic pressures: _____

_____

CUSTOMERS AND COMPETITION

Customers play a key role in this analysis. What do your current customers tell you about your service/products? What do those who are not your customers say?

Strategic alliances and competitors can teach you a lot about opportunities and threats. Who really is your competition? What are the strengths and weaknesses of the competition? In what ways are they unique?

Customers and Competition Analysis

Current customers: _____

_____

What do your current customers tell you about your service/products?

_____

_____

What do those who are not your customers say? _____

_____

Who are your key strategic alliances? _____

_____

Who are your competitors?_____

_____

How are they unique? _____

_____

STRENGTHS AND WEAKNESSES

An organization's resources, capabilities and core competencies are critical in creating a future. There are often more opportunities than an organization can respond to. A knowledge of your strengths will help you keep focused and see new opportunities for business. A candid assessment of weaknesses will inject a dose of reality into your planning.

	Strengths	**Weaknesses**
1.	_____	_____
2.	_____	_____
3.	_____	_____
4.	_____	_____
5.	_____	_____
6.	_____	_____
7.	_____	_____
8.	_____	_____

CRITICAL ISSUES OF THE FUTURE

The identification of four critical issues will help in the visioning process. It may be helpful to state each issue in the form of a question that can be answered. For example: How can our focus on past technical capability be used to launch current efforts?

Critical Issues of the Future

1. _____
   _____
   _____

2. _____
   _____
   _____

3. _____
   _____
   _____

4. _____
   _____
   _____

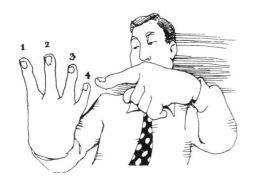

S T E P

3

Define the Mission

CHECKING YOUR MISSION

Your first obligation is to find out the mission you are meant for . . . . Your mission will manifest in you when you decide to listen to your heart's desire.

—Naomi Stephen, Finding Your Life Mission

Individuals have reasons for living their lives. A personal mission statement articulates an individual's unique direction. A personal mission articulates what you do, the purpose for which you exist. It answers the existential question, *''What is it I'm here to do?''*

Defining your personal mission acts as an emotional touchstone that unleashes powerful feelings. A mission is not a narrow goal, but an overall guiding direction. Sometimes people do not want to clarify their mission for fear they will be held to it. A personal mission is not a restraint but fuel, propelling you toward your vision.

The following questions are helpful in guiding an individual in the process of developing a personal mission. It is best to have a few uninterrupted hours to work through the personal mission section.

Develop Your Own Personal Mission

What is my basic purpose in the work that I do? _____

_____

What is my basic purpose in life? _____

_____

What are the unique aspects that I bring to work? _____

_____

What values are most important to what I do? _____

_____

What are the critical considerations that I make (i.e., family, community, geographic location, etc.) when I develop my mission? _____

_____

LINK TO PERSONAL MASTERY

A mission answers the reason you are alive, your core existential reason for being on the planet. A mission is often not the first answer to the question, Why? When a group of nuclear technicians was asked what they did, they said, ''We build bombs.'' To have stayed with that answer would have produced a less than inspiring mission. By asking, ''Why? again and again, the group got to the reason they did their work–to learn to use science and technology to serve the needs of the nation. That mission was one that could keep them going.

Use the worksheet below to distill your understanding of your mission to its essence.

Personal Mission Worksheet

What do you say is your mission? _____

_____

Why do you say that? _____

_____

What is the true purpose of what you do? _____

_____

Now take some time to revise your personal mission based on what you discovered above.

My Personal Mission Statement

_____

_____

_____

_____

_____

_____

Mission Buffers Stress

Research has shown that people who have an understanding or reason for what they are doing, do much better in times of stress. This sense of coherence or mission helps people focus and endure challenges that stand in the way of their realizing their vision. With a clear mission, people know what is important to them and can focus their activity. They can be strategic and pick priorities, rather than be reactive.

Mission Drives Strategy

A change in mission resulted when the leaders of Federal Express decided that they were in the transportation business rather than in the package delivery business. To align their business with this new mission required two large changes.

1. Rethinking the assumption that packages should travel the shortest distance between pickup and delivery points to a system whereby all packages are flown to a hub city (Memphis, Tennessee) and sorted and redirected for their final delivery.

2. The need to develop a new and dedicated information system that allowed the company to have concrete real-time information on the whereabouts of every package.*

---

* Beckhand, R., and W. Pritchard. *Changing the Essense: The Art of Creating and Leading Fundamental Change in Organizations.* Jossey-Bass, 1992, p. 39

ORGANIZATIONAL OR TEAM MISSION STATEMENTS

Organizational missions are collections of personal missions. The process of matching individual and organizational missions often makes the difference between a high performing organization and one that is just getting by. When people find an organization that is a vehicle for their personal mission, their energy and excitement are multiplied.

The answer to questions about the mission comes out of analysis that a group goes through to find out who it is. The analysis is built upon the environmental scan and usually requires more than a single session.

The mission emerges from a process of asking for feedback from customers and employees and then comparing it to internal views of what the organization thinks it is doing. In many cases the organization thinks its mission is clear until people analyze the work that they do. Sometimes an organization's work does not fit the mission for which it was intended. Revisiting the mission can strengthen the resolve of the people in the organization.

Mission Is a Core Competency

How you define the mission of your business determines the way that you structure your business. For example, one way to see the mission of the railroad is that it maintains the railroad; another way is to see it as engaged in the freight transfer business.

At the core of an organization is its purpose or mission. The mission provides the guiding direction for developing strategy, defining critical success factors, seaching out key opportunities, making resource allocation choices and pleasing customers or stakeholders.

The mission is the synthesis of what the customers see as your business, what the employees in your group see as your business, what your products and services should be, who your customers are and what value you bring to them. It also includes what the larger environment sees as your purpose and what work you actually do. It is built upon your core values.

Mission Describes Uniqueness

Your mission statement should distinguish your business from others, making clear what is unique about what you do. It tells, from the customer's perspective, what you offer. The mission statement is a guiding tool for the employees of the organization. It helps them make decisions and know what course of action to take. It provides a consistent focus from which the visioning process proceeds.

An Organizational Mission Must Have:

What you do: _____

_____

_____

For whom: _____

_____

_____

Your uniqueness: _____

_____

_____

To synthesize a group or team mission builds on the individual missions and the analysis of opportunities and threats already conducted. Once the organization has defined what it really does and the purpose for which it exists, the mission statement becomes easy. The specific statement is an outcome of lots of prework.

ORGANIZATIONAL OR TEAM MISSION STATEMENTS (continued)

Developing a Team Mission

A team mission is just an extension of the individual mission process. When you bring the development of the mission to a group or departmental level, it's important to discuss not just the systems or procedures they use, but their unique contribution.

Missions work best when they are grounded in the past and project that past into the future. They become more essential and inspiring when they focus less on what you do, and more on what you will do for your key customers, how you will affect them. For example, the following represent mission statements of two very different organizations. Can you guess what each one does?

Our mission is to

- *Prevent Harm*

- *Survive*

- *Be Nice*

—Phoenix Fire Department

"By defining and solving problems of the working and healing environments, we aim to improve the quality of our customers' lives and become their reference point for quality and service. Through personal competence, participation, research, and design, we strive for excellence in each aspect of our business."

—*Herman Miller*
manufacturer of high-quality chairs

Use the following worksheet to map the information that will help you develop your group mission.

Organizational Mission Worksheet

What business(s) are you in? _____

_____

Who are your customers? _____

_____

What added value do customers of your company/group receive? _____

_____

What contribution is your company/group making to the society as a whole?

_____

_____

What is your company/group especially good at? (products/service/strength)

_____

_____

How is it distinctive and unique? _____

_____

EXAMPLES OF MISSION STATEMENTS

ORGANIZATIONAL OR TEAM MISSION STATEMENTS (continued)

To give you an example of how reworking the mission of an organization can give it more energy, review the following examples.

The Sierra Club

Before

The mission of the Sierra Club is to influence public, private and corporate policies and actions through Club programs at the local, national and international levels.

After

Building on generations of success, the Sierra Club inspires people to join in protecting earth's natural treasures and vitality. Through the club, individuals magnify their power to restore the places where they live and preserve the places they love.

Berryessa Union School District

Before

The Berryessa School District is dedicated to serving the educational needs of pupils within the community. The board of trustees, staff members and the state share in the responsibilities for the education of pupils. The commitment is to provide a free public education to maintain a literate populace, which is the basis for a democratic society.

After

In Berryessa Union District, we are committed to providing the necessary resources and inspiration for each student to develop

A command of learning
Social responsibility
Critical thinking

We are dedicated to motivating students to achieve their maximum potential and to value lifelong learning.

Mission or Vision—Which Is First?

Many groups have experimented with developing an image of the future—their vision—without referring to their mission. What tends to happen is that the image becomes impractical when it is not grounded in the specific mission of the organization. Because the mission statement is directly linked to a broad analysis of the customers and environment, it makes sense imagining the future in the context of the mission, because it comes from information.

Often groups will generate their images of the future without being informed by the customer. In these cases the visioning process can get off track. An image of the future that is viewed as too outrageous or the gaps created between an unlikely image of the future and where the organization is currently deplete organizational energy. The perception is that the gap is too wide to cross.

On the other hand, sometimes the group or organization needs to extend itself into a new arena. In that case it would make sense to do the image of the future first to establish a stretch of intention. The group would then focus on creating their mission afterward so that it focuses them on their future.

PITFALLS IN CREATING MISSION STATEMENTS

Stay away from crafting the words of the mission too much. Make sure the statement evokes feeling and passion. The statement should say who you are and why you're passionate about it. Put your attention toward a broad focus on the spirit of what you do. Make it short—*try not to have more than three sentences.*

In some cases the vision was created as the carrier of the emotion and the mission was the practical action statement. What happens in these cases is that the mission doesn't carry enough weight to keep people moving through all the steps of what it takes to get to the vision.

A mission evokes a personal response. Work on it until it gets to be so clear that reminding yourself of it will keep you, on a really bad day, from walking out and quitting.

Clarifying your mission is not a risk-free enterprise—it can often increase an individual's frustration with his current situation and where he or she would like to be. When some people talk about mission, they revisit past experiences of disappointment and disillusionment. Their willingness to take part in dreaming again sometimes takes an act of courage.

Slogans or Missions

There is difference between slogans and mission statements. A slogan may be something like:

"We are customer obsessed."

"All students can learn; all students can achieve, always."

Slogans such as these focus attention, but they don't communicate a sense of the purpose for the organization. Why is the group customer obsessed? Slogans do not carry the enduring power that a mission does.

Missions . . . Too Many Missions

Some organizations have developed successive mission statements and none of them seem to stick. Often this is because the missions were created quickly without the organization's support. In some cases the mission did not get at the core of what the business was really about. Try asking:

What would we do if 70 percent of our resources were taken away?

_____

_____

_____

Would the company be doing this anyway?

_____

_____

_____

A restaurant team that answered that question found that what they really would be doing was entertainment rather than the food service business.

Gaining Commitment Through Involvement

Those who craft the process own it. In the development of the mission, it is important to understand that you will probably go through several drafts. Each draft should be reviewed by as many people in the organization as possible, including key stakeholders. One way to do this is to have a design team consisting of representatives of the groups within the organization draft the mission; then a larger group, often everybody, tests and critiques the document. The design team then synthesizes the feedback in a single mission.

After this, it is common to do visioning with as large a group as possible. It is important at this stage to include people who have not been part of the design team. It is common for the design team to have been meeting for several months before the visioning starts.

4

Create a Vision

PICTURING EXCELLENCE

I believe in intuition and inspiration . . . at times I feel certain that I am right while not knowing the reason . . . imagination is more important than knowledge. For knowledge is limited, whereas imagination embraces the entire world, stimulating progress, giving birth to evolution.

—Albert Einstein, scientist

A vision is a powerful mental image of what we want to create in the future. It reflects what we care about most, represents an expression of what our mission will look like and is harmonious with our values and sense of purpose. Visions are the result of head and heart working together. They are rooted in reality, but focus on the future. They enable us to explore possibilities, desired realities. Because of this, they become a framework for what we want to create, which guides us in making choices and commitments for action.

Even though vision directs us toward the future, it is important to understand that it is experienced in the present. The tension that comes from comparing the image of a desired future with today's reality is what fuels a vision to action. Powerful visions are never an escape from reality. It is important that an awareness of today's reality be present in a vision or else it becomes disconnected and powerless.

Defining Vision

- An image of how we see our purpose unfolding

- A picture of the preferred future we seek to create

- An answer to the question "What do we really want?"

PICTURING EXCELLENCE (continued)

Vision Is a Compass

Use your vision as a compass. It can guide you when all other indicators of direction seem to be gone. Visions are strongest when they focus on an image that has enduring capability. Visions help individuals and groups make sense of what is going on by stressing the core competencies on which constant improvement can be built.

The Vision Is a Stretch

As the whole organization works together to create a vision, it is not a plan, it's a stretch. It is important to extend your vision just a little farther than you think you can go. Little visions are not worth committing 10 years of your life to create.

Vision Map

A vision is created from the fundamental values of the individuals in the organization, the fundamental purpose, and awareness of the current reality, coming together to produce a shared future.

Each group experiences its visioning process in a different way. On the next page is a map of one organization's process of developing a vision.

EXAMPLE AHEAD

Visioning Process

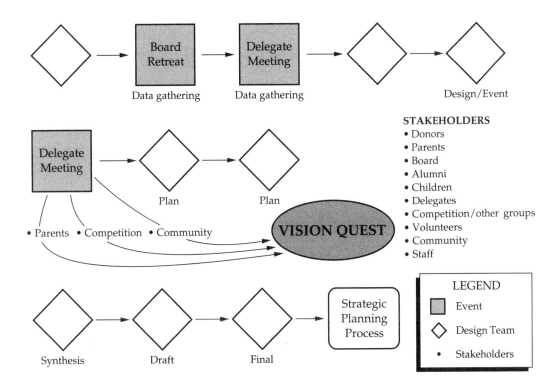

Vision Endures

Visions capture minds, hearts and spirits, giving people a higher purpose for their actions. A vision paints a picture of how the organization will be in the future. A vision tends to evolve but needs to be big enough so it does not change substantially every few years.

Visions Handoff to Planning

The planning process starts with where you are and asks for specific incremental steps. Creating an image of excellence starts with a bigger, more inspirational view and then employs planning to work backward, identifying the steps that would need to be taken to create such a future. Planning has often failed to catalyze results because it tends not to create the excitement and energy that an image of excellence does.

VISION AND PERFORMANCE

I could detect a distinct correlation between the notion of vision and performance. The good ones had a vision. As for the bad ones, it was hard to tell why the people had come to work that morning.

—Donald Povesil, Vice President, Corporate Planning, Westinghouse

One of the key qualities of high-performance organizations and teams is that they have a clear picture of what they are trying to create together. A vision statement captures in words or pictures the desired future of your organization. Creating the passion and commitment of aligned actions is at the core of managing a fast-changing environment. The key to this aligned action is a shared vision. It acts like a magnet that pulls all the people together toward the same direction. It is not a one-time process that employees engage in and then forget. It is a skill that is learned and used repeatedly—the process that evokes more creative solutions to business challenges.

A vision statement should include your basic strategy on how you want to achieve your mission. It should include your spoken and unspoken hopes and dreams. Your vision should inspire and touch you. If it does not inspire you, it will probably not inspire others. A vision comes from within and from without. Developing it is sometimes a messy process, and living it becomes a daily challenge.

VISIONING RELEASES SPIRIT

Vision is not just one of the six New Age skills, it is the pivotal skill. The scenarios you build with vision help put your future in focus, allowing you to convert potential dangers into opportunities. Visionary executives not only position their organizations to make the most of impending changes, they attempt to influence those changes by causing rather than merely reacting to them.

— **Craig R. Hickman and Michael A. Silva, Creating Excellence**

When groups vision, they release the spirit of the organization. Spirit is derived from the Latin spiare—''to breathe.'' When a person or group has a vision, it seems to have more energy. Vision breathes life into the group and provides the basis for inspiration. Visions are the product of the head and heart working together.

Visions Again

With the emphasis on visioning in business in the past decade, many people have had the experience of creating vision statements without learning to experience vision. Some managers think that a vision is just a dream, a flight from reality, wishful thinking, naive idealism or merely ideal fantasy—in other words, not central to the business of business.

What organizations are often missing is the emotional power and energy that is catalyzed when people have a shared vision. For an organization to become vision driven requires a clear understanding about the values on which the individuals and teams base their actions.

THE VISION-REFINING PROCESS

VISIONING RELEASES SPIRIT (continued)

Thinking Differently

Creating an image of excellence requires individuals or groups first to expand their thinking and then narrow in and focus on how to accomplish the vision.

The first phase, known as divergent thinking, involves opening up your mind to new possibilities and unusual ways of thinking. It involves seeing unconnected events or trends as connected. After thinking in a divergent way it is necessary to engage in convergent thinking, to bring together trends and analyze their impact and create a format for selecting action steps. Convergent thinking refines the alternatives and leads to effective decision making.

Divergent Imaging

Think of an issue, challenge or problem and place it in the center of the circle below. On the space surrounding, write as many ideas as you can about approaching, solving or coping with this. Let your mind wander. Draw pictures, shapes or figures of all the things you can think of that might, even peripherally, have something to do with this issue. This process is very different from brainstorming, because most of the ideas generated this way tend to be short-term goals, not images.

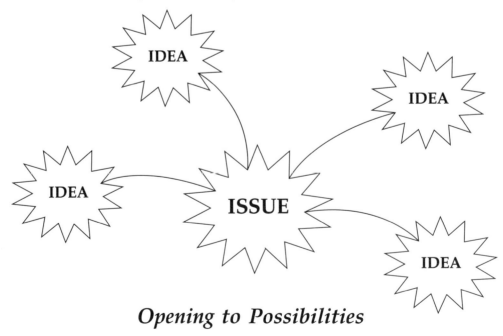

Opening to Possibilities

Convergent Imaging

Now that you have all the images collected, look them over and ask yourself, what is an overall image that combines the best of these ideas? Bringing these divergent ideas into a single image can often provide a powerful direction for communication of the vision.

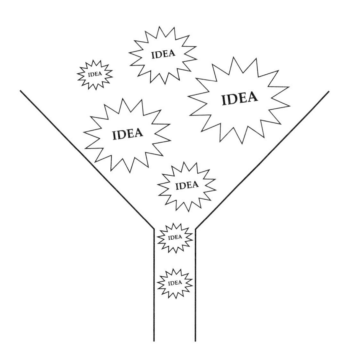

FOCUSING THE IMAGE

THE POWER OF PREFERRED IMAGERY

By believing passionately in something that still does not exist, we create it. The nonexistent is whatever we have not sufficiently desired.

—Nikos Kazantsakis

The mind is a powerful organ. It is possible to think of past memories and have them affect your physiology. For example, if you were to think of a past experience that was stressful or upsetting, you might find that your heart beats faster, your palms start to perspire or your neck muscles get tighter. All these reactions come from *remembering* the image, not having the actual experience.

If a negative image can evoke uncomfortable experiences, shouldn't a positive image bring about an enhanced state of being? In fact, the body can't tell the difference between what is real or imagined. Therefore, it is important to pay attention to what your mind is focused on.

What memory do you have that evokes a positive feeling?

_____

_____

What memory do you have that evokes a negative feeling?

_____

_____

Experiencing Vision

People experience vision in different ways: some see mental images, some experience them as sensations, others just have an unspoken sense of what they are. When people, teams or organizations generate a vision, they most commonly refer to the vision as a powerful mental image of what they want to create in the future.

Visions Defined

A vision is a picture of a preferred future state, a description of what it would like to be some years from now. It is a dynamic picture of the future. It is more than a dream or set of hopes; it is a commitment. The vision provides the context for designing and managing the changes that will be necessary to reach those goals.

Visions are rooted in reality but focused on the future. They enable us to explore possibilities. They are desired realities. While vision directs us toward the future, it is experienced in the present.

Cautions

Creating an image of a preferred future is not a risk-free enterprise—the gap between where you are now and where you want to be can increase frustration. Sometimes people don't want to vision because they think it will just make them unhappy with where they are. This tension is a natural outcome of creating a gap between now and the future.

Sometimes individuals, groups or organizations stop short of their vision because the tension is too upsetting. What may be helpful at this point is not to lower the expectation, but to allow a longer time to achieve the vision. In this way a more lofty vision can be achieved. Being able to live with this tension will allow the individual, group or organization to reach their vision more successfully. This is one of the hallmarks of a learning individual or organization.

Some people have even experienced the creation of a vision as manipulation: they were coerced into a process that was not to their liking. This situation can come about when people are involved in a visioning process that produces a wide gap between where they are now and where they are asked to stretch. It's important to remind people that no one can give anyone else a vision.

HOW TO BEGIN

Visioning works best if it is not used to focus on specific outcomes; i.e., increased market share, stockholder value, etc., but instead on developing an organization, group or personal work that has more life, meaning and direction and nourishes creative potential. Visions gather more momentum when they focus on how people will interact with each other or serve their customers or society in unique ways.

Include Others

Cast the net of participation widely. Have discussions with customers, suppliers, community representatives, employees from other groups, etc. What do they see as your optimal future? Don't leave any group out; everyone's perspective is important. Collect stories that tell about the dreams of the people in your organization.

Who should be included in your vision process? _____

_____

Move Beyond the Numbers

Inspiring visions are not about numbers, earnings per share or return on investment. People become enthusiastic about being the best, the highest quality or most innovative. Include enough stretch so the vision will be a challenge and reason for working together.

Qualities of a Vision

- It motivates, inspires
- It is a stretch, moves towards greatness
- It is clear, concrete
- It is achievable, not a fantasy
- It fits with the highest values
- It is easy to communicate, clear and simple

Remember Your Past Experiences

Most everyone has had an experience of creating a vision or being part of a group that did. Chances are you can still remember these experiences, even if they happened long ago.

▶ List past experiences you had with visioning.

_____

_____

_____

_____

▶ What was so memorable about these experiences?

_____

_____

_____

_____

▶ How did these experiences start?

_____

_____

_____

_____

▶ What sustained them?

_____

_____

_____

_____

HOW TO BEGIN (continued)

How Many to Include

Example #1

A representative group from the organization uses one or more of the visioning tools and prepares a draft of the mission and vision statements and then circulates the drafts to the rest of the organization for comment.

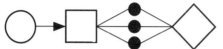

Example #2

A representative group uses one or more of the visioning tools to respond to a series of questions about the mission and vision. This group then engages other important groups in the organization with the visioning tools, a draft is created and then re-circulated to groups for their input and feedback. After these meetings, the responses are brought together by the vision group or members of the other group and then the draft is circulated for comment.

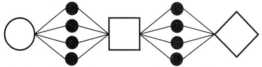

The first example has the advantage of being faster and less time consuming. It also generates less buy-in and excitement. The second example increases the amount of input and buy-in from the organization, but it does take more time and gives you more data to assess.

Leading With Vision

If you are the leader of a new team, begin to formulate your vision quickly. As time goes by, you lose your opportunity to make changes. In many instances, people say that the first 100 days is the most important time to involve people, refocus and make changes.

Key to above diagrams:

◯ Representative Group Uses Visioning Tools

☐ Draft Prepared

⣿ Important Subgroups

◇ Final Vision Statement

VISIONING TOOLS

Creating a vision is best approached in an expanded state of consciousness. There are many ways to go beyond the everyday, conscious thought process. These processes start with inviting people to reconnect with their hopes for the future. These tools require some time to allow the divergent and convergent thinking to take place.

> ## *TOOLS FOR VISIONING*
>
> IMAGERY
> SYMBOLS
> STORY TELLING
> PHYSICAL CHALLENGE

Imagery

Imagery invites you to use your mind to take you to a time in the future when you have accomplished your vision. Imagery is the mental process of creating sights, sounds, smells, tastes and sensations in the absence of any external stimuli. Imagery is a means of improving communication between the conscious and unconscious levels of the mind.

Imagery gives you the power to span time. Imagery is less susceptible to personal censorship and can sometimes be more revealing than verbal expression, allowing the expression of ideas and feelings. Imagery is an especially useful tool when facing tasks that are complex, uncertain and innovative.

Imagery is enhanced with a relaxed state of mind. To begin the visioning process, sit in a comfortable position. Allow some time to dream; let your mind wander to "remember" the future. There is no right way to do this. The focus is to get a clear experience of what this time will be like. Allow the mind to move from focusing on all the business details to a time in the future.

Organizational Vision, Values and Mission

VISIONING TOOLS (continued)

Imagine yourself, your team or organization three to five years from now, receiving an award for an accomplishment. What is the award for? What has been accomplished?

_____

_____

_____

_____

_____

Another way to image the future is to select one of the company's or group's key values and allow yourself to imagine how you personally embody this value from the moment you walk into your office until you return home in the evening.

_____

_____

_____

_____

_____

Symbols

The soul never thinks without a picture.

—Aristotle

Symbols are pictures or images that represent the vision. These are not artistic, carefully crafted pictures, but representations that mirror an image of the future. Each person can draw an image of what the vision would look like. With a large group, you might want to have someone take all the images and pull them together into an integrative symbol. You might want to use crayons, flip chart paper, colored pens, tape, scissors and other supplies to create a group image from the individual images that you have created.

Draw a symbol that represents a way of showing where you will be when you accomplish your vision.

Story Telling

Sometimes it makes sense to create an enactment of the vision of the future. In this way people can have a direct experience of the dialogue, actions and behaviors that will be needed to make the vision real.

For example, to help a group understand the meaning of its vision, ask members to create a play that shows how the organization would look when the vision is accomplished. For comic relief you can also ask people to portray how it is now. For example, how would a person get promoted in the visioned organization as compared to now?

Physical Challenge

Often physically active experiences can release people from their usual patterns of thinking. Many games and outdoor activities can involve individuals and groups in new ways of thinking. Often the exercise is set up in a way to allow the individual or team to think differently about how they solve the challenge.

OVERALL VISIONING PROCESS

Guidelines for Visioning

- Allow yourself to be in a relaxed state, where there is no pressure
- Focus on what really matters to you
- Focus on what you want to create, not how to make it happen
- Focus on imagining what is happening
- Avoid focus on today's problems and what isn't working

Vision Questions

- If we could be what we wanted in five years, what would we be?
- How would we know we were there?
- What would be a stretch for ourselves?
- What kind of organization do we want to be?
- What do we really want to do or create?
- What would be worth committing to over the next 10 years?
- How do we differentiate ourselves from our competition?
- What are the right things to do?

Time Line

Set a horizon and focus your thinking using one or more of the visioning tools to help you focus on where you would like the organization or group to be; for example, in the year 2000.

What vision are you creating for the next:

- Two years: _____

- Five years: _____

- Ten years: _____

To help you collect your ideas you might use this framework.

Vision Worksheet

	Now	Future
Business or products	_____	_____
Markets	_____	_____
Key relationships	_____	_____
Organizational capability	_____	_____
Culture	_____	_____
Competencies	_____	_____
Processes	_____	_____
Behavior	_____	_____
Structure	_____	_____
Mission	_____	_____

Visions should be expressed in the present tense. Say, "We are." Using "we will" or "we shall" only reinforces the gap between the present and the future. Expressing the future state in present tense forces the question of how to emerge, with the creative tension that puts the vision into action.

Avoid Competition

It is best to avoid the competitive phrases of being first, number one or the best, because these statements tend to move an organization forward and then, when accomplished, leave the group without a next step. This approach can also have the negative effect of focusing the group to defend their #1 position and reduce learning and innovation.

A Powerful Vision Statement

- Presents where we want to go
- Easy to read and understand
- Captures the desired spirit of the organization
- Dynamically incomplete so people can fill in the pieces
- Compact—can be used to guide decision making
- Gets people's attention
- Describes a preferred and meaningful future state
- Can be felt/experienced/gives people goose bumps when they hear it
- Gives people a better understanding of how their individual purpose could be realized in the group or company
- Provides a motivating force, even in hard times
- Is perceived as achievable
- Is challenging and compelling, stretching beyond what is comfortable

---

After you have finished visioning, it is time to refine the output and work on identifying the gaps between the reality of today and the picture of the future.

Example of Vision

We are committed to being conscious of our values both individually and as a team:

To be healthy and promote health

To be honest with our patients and with one another

To be broadminded, creative and to have the courage to stretch our capabilities.

To be recognized and compensated for our abilities, achievements and advancements.

And to enjoy our freedom.

Les Plack, DDS—Dental Office

S T E P

5

Implement the Vision

COMMUNICATING THE VISION

When the diverse elements of the organization are aligned, the energy is focused and the capacity for concerted action improved . . . . Priorities become clear, and the contributions of each employee are maximized.

—Laura Spencer, Winning Through Participation

The communication of the vision to other groups is a very important step in the development of an aligned organization. It is important at this stage to give an opportunity to the people who have not been directly involved in the visioning process to have an opportunity to discuss the vision, clarify common meanings of the words used and find ways to understand how this vision will affect what they do. It is a time to focus on listening and clarifying, not defending the vision.

When setting a vision for an entire organization, it is important that top management lead a formal organization-wide communication process to establish the vision as a tenant of the organization.

Participating creates alignment, as members help to shape, and therefore commonly own, the shared vision. This alignment brings a sense of unity and cooperation, resulting in new levels of trust and teamwork. Communication is enhanced within and between departments and levels of the organization, thus creating the conditions in which creativity flourishes. All of this results in improved organizational effectiveness.

COMMUNICATING THE VISION (continued)

Getting Organizational Feedback

After the vision has been clarified, take what your group has developed, go to the next level in the organization and get feedback on what your vision represents. Look for gaps. After this feedback is gathered, the vision often needs to be reworked and the plans for its implementation begin to take place.

A force field analysis is a helpful tool at this point. List all the forces that are working to make the vision happen and all the forces that are keeping it from happening.

To create a force field, make two lists: 1) of all the forces that are keeping the vision from being implemented, and 2) all the forces that are helping the vision become reality.

There are three types of forces:

1. Things that have to do with individuals

2. Things that have to do with other people or groups

3. Things of a nonpersonal nature, cultural assumptions, environment, etc.

Force Field Analysis

Forces that are keeping the vision from being implemented:

_____

_____

Forces that are helping the vision become reality:

_____

_____

It is easier to remove restraining forces than to increase the positive forces. The vision can then be incorporated into the strategic planning process by becoming a key element in guiding the choice of strategic options the group faces.

Planning to Implement Vision

Planning at the end of a visioning process sets the stage for the process of determining what an organization or group intends to be in the future and how it will get there. The visioning process has allowed you to find the best future and now it's time to create the best path to reach that destination.

Implementation Questions

- How do we get to the desired state?

- How will we know when we get there?

- What is going to help or hinder us?

- What strategies and programs are needed?

- What should we keep doing/stop doing?

- How will we know how it is going?

- How will the implementation effort be conducted?

- What are the implementation phases?

- What have we learned from our experience?

LIVING THE VISION

A long, dusty road stretches between the vision and its implementation. One of the hardest things is to live with the inconsistencies along the way. As a vision gets spread out in a group, there will be lots of opportunity for poking holes in the vision. The visions that are most vehemently declared often fall prey to the biggest bouts of hypocrisy. It is best to spend time getting your own house in order so that your internal behavior doesn't look too different when people compare it to your espoused vision.

Process Not Declaration

Expect and prepare for some inconsistencies, admit them and show how living the vision is a process, not a declaration. The learning is in the humble application and reapplication of the vision to daily choice and action. A strong vision helps people make decisions and guides their thinking when discrepancy arises. Stay away from the plaques and cards until you are well on your way to internalizing the vision.

Leaders' Role

Visions are lived in the details, the everyday choices. Many leaders err in thinking that as long as they have the big picture, the details don't matter. It is the details of the execution of the vision that everyone sees. Trust is built from repeatable behavior. If people are to trust in the vision, they need to see it informing choices, policies and actions in the organization.

Part of living the vision is making people aware of its application to action. The leaders of the vision need to be ready to declare over and over again its importance and application. This short vision speech helps people focus their attention and gives them an energy boost. The role of the leader is to remind them of their dedication and commitment to achieving the vision. It's also helpful if in this speech the leader can use specific examples of how people are living the vision, which creates a new set of stories about the organization's or team's capacity to manifest the vision.

A vision is a visceral experience. It should evoke goose bumps in you and give you a feeling of being compelled to do something. A leader without emotion will have a hard time leading his or her team in the vision. A vision needs to be experienced emotionally because that is the way people change their behavior. People don't change from rational reasons but from emotional experiences. The leader's ability to evoke an emotional connection to the vision will enhance its ability to take hold.

Some Dangers

Visions are set to inspire constant evolutionary change. The vision must give people a sense about what they are working for to allow them to take risks to achieve it. At times a vision can become so static that it impedes change; it no longer pushes the team or the organization forward. At times like these, a vision may have been accomplished and needs to be refreshed. Then groups from the outside can ask questions about the vision and inspire the internal group to look again.

Refreshing a vision is often painful for the organization. It requires the ability to look at assumptions that have been held as truth. These past success patterns can hold the vision hostage.

A vision should focus on creating an inspired environment inside the organization first and serving the customer second. Research has shown that how the employees are treated inside the organization is how they treat customers. Therefore, if the visioning process is focused outside only, it is hard to imagine uninspired people providing inspired service.

Visioning Links to Organizational Change

Visioning often produces organizational change. When an organization or team sees a greater sense of possibilities, it then experiences the dissonance associated with the gap between where it is and where it wants to be. If this tension can be seen as a rubber band, pulling the potential of the group upward, then the tension can be managed. If the tension pulls the aspirations of the group down, then energy decreases and burnout sets in.

If the tension between where it is and where it wants to be is too large, the gap demotivates people as well. Each group and individual needs to determine how much tension is tolerable. This level probably differs at different times in the life cycle of the organization and the individual. Growth seems to be a process of increasing the tension of where you can go and then closing the gap with work and plans.

LIVING THE VISION (continued)

Honor the Past

Effective visions prepare for the future but honor the past. No one likes to think of his or her past as having been a wrong way. People who are ashamed of their past tend not to stretch far into the future. On the other hand, people who can accept their actions and see how they were stepping stones to the current reality can change more easily. In other words, change does not come from making people feel bad about their past. Change occurs in creating a continuity from the past to the future. Honoring the past provides the springboard for moving forward.

Anchoring the Vision

One way to make sure that the vision is translated into real action is to add the values and key elements of the vision to the performance evaluation system. General Electric did this with its top 100 officers. Each of them was rated on a scale of one to five in terms of how they supported the company's core values.

How does your company support its key values with performance evaluation?

_____

_____

Incentives:

_____

_____

Reward structures:

_____

_____

OUTCOMES OF VISIONING PROCESS

The following outcomes have been reported by individuals, groups and organizations that have completed a visioning process.

1. Alignment

People and groups that go through the visioning process have an increased sense of purpose and an overall congruence with the organization's goals. There is an increased sense of energy and excitement. Work has a deeper meaning in groups that have visioned.

2. Empowerment

Visioning increases the sense of personal mastery, group empowerment and organizational vigor. The experience of taking direct responsibility for outcomes they have crafted increases the ability to act.

3. Respect

Personal visioning provides a framework for appreciating strengths and putting action in perspective. Visioning provides a ground for shared participation, and all contributions are treated equally in a team process. For a team or organization, a shared vision is an image, like a recipe, around which everyone can contribute their own ingredients.

4. Interdependence

Group visioning is a format for groups to experience how they are connected at a higher level with other groups in the organization. It gives a bigger picture in which to place individual efforts. Visioning highlights the paradox between being connected to a larger effort and making individual choice.

5. Innovation

Groups and individuals that have worked through a visioning process have increased their ability to generate divergent ideas of the future. They have stretched their ability to think beyond short-term goals and imagine alternative futures. This ability to generate visions and move toward them is a primary determinant of success.

6. Commitment

Groups or individuals who have experienced guiding themselves through visioning notice that their vision often replaces rules as a standard of guidance. The vision is used to make decisions and focus attention. The role of supervision comes from within. People work not from compliance, but from commitment.

SUMMARY

The process of clarifying values, mission and vision is both a personal and organizational task. You don't have to wait for the leadership of your company to begin this process. Answer for yourself: What do I want to be? What are my capabilities to do this? and What do I want to be known for? There is no better time than now to start.

GO FOR IT!

REFERENCES

Beckhard, R. & W. Pritchard. *Changing the Essence: The Art of Creating and Leading Fundamental Change in Organizations.* Jossey-Bass, 1992.

Jaffe, Dennis, Cynthia Scott, and Esther Orioli. "Visionary Leadership: Moving a Company from Burnout to Inspired Performance." In Adams, John D. (ed.) *Transforming Leadership: From Vision to Results.* Alexandria, VA. Miles River Press, 1986.

Jaffe, Dennis and Cynthia Scott. *Take This Job and Love It.* New York: Simon & Schuster, 1988.

Hickman, Craig R. and Michael A. Silva. *Creating Excellence: Managing Corporate Culture, Strategy and Change in the New Age.* New York: New American Library, 1984.

Parker, Marjorie. *Creating Shared Vision.* Clarendon Hills, IL.: Dialog International, 1990.

Rokeach, M. A. and S. J. Ball-Rokeach. *American Psychologist.* 1989, May p. 775–784.

Schmidt, Warren H. & Barry Z. Posner. *Managerial Values in Perspective.* American Management Associates, 1983.

Scott, Cynthia and Dennis Jaffe. *Empowerment: Building High Commitment Workplaces.* Menlo Park, CA: Crisp Publications, 1992.

Spencer, Laura. *Winning Through Participation.* Dubuque, Iowa: Kendall/Hunt Publishing Co., 1989.

NOTES

NOTES

NOTES

NOTES

NOTES

NOTES

NOTES

NOTES

OVER 150 BOOKS AND 35 VIDEOS AVAILABLE IN THE 50-MINUTE SERIES

We hope you enjoyed this book. If so, we have good news for you. This title is part of the best-selling *50-MINUTE*™ *Series* of books. All *Series* books are similar in size and identical in price. Many are supported with training videos.

To order *50-MINUTE* Books and Videos or request a free catalog, contact your local distributor or Crisp Publications, Inc., 1200 Hamilton Court, Menlo Park, CA 94025. Our toll-free number is (800) 442-7477.

50-Minute Series Books and Videos Subject Areas . . .

Management
Training
Human Resources
Customer Service and Sales Training
Communications
Small Business and Financial Planning
Creativity
Personal Development
Wellness
Adult Literacy and Learning
Career, Retirement and Life Planning

Other titles available from Crisp Publications in these categories

Crisp Computer Series
The Crisp Small Business & Entrepreneurship Series
Quick Read Series
Management
Personal Development
Retirement Planning

heartwork **VALUES CARDS**℠	**ALWAYS VALUED**	**OFTEN VALUED**	**SOMETIMES VALUED**
SELDOM VALUED	**LEAST VALUED**	**Fairness** ▲ Similar opportunity, respecting everyone's rights	**Honesty** ▲ Sincere, truthful
Tolerance ▲ Respectful of others	**Courageous** ▲ Standing up for your beliefs, overcoming fear	**Integrity** ▲ Acting in line with your beliefs	**Forgiveness** ▲ Able to pardon others and let go of hurt
Peace ▲ End of war, non-violent conflict resolution	**Environment** ▲ Respecting the future of the Earth	**Challenge** ❤ Testing physical limits, strength, speed and agility	**Self-Acceptance** ❤ Self-respect, Self-esteem

Knowledge ❤ Seeking intellectual stimulation, new ideas, truth and understanding	**Adventure** ❤ Challenge, risk-taking, testing limits	**Creativity** ❤ Finding new ways to do things, innovative	**Personal Growth** ❤ Continual learning, development of new skills, self-awareness
Inner Harmony ❤ Freedom from inner conflict, integrated, whole	**Spiritual Growth** ❤ Relationship to higher purpose, divine being	**Belonging** ☎ Being connected to and liked by others	**Diplomacy** ☎ Finding common ground with difficult people and situations, resolving conflict
Teamwork ☎ Cooperating with others toward a common goal	**Helping** ☎ Taking care of others, doing what they need	**Communication** ☎ Open dialogue, exchange of views	**Friendship** ☎ Close companionship, on-going relationships
Consensus ☎ Making decisions everyone can live with	**Respectful** ☎ Showing consideration, regarding with honor	**Tradition** ✛ Respecting the way things have always been done	**Security** ✛ Freedom from worry, safe, risk free

Stability ✛	**Neatness** ✛	**Self-Control** ✛	**Perseverance** ✛
Certainty, predictability	Tidy, orderly, clean	Self-disciplined, restrained	Pushing through to the end, completing tasks
Rationality ✛	**Health** ✳	**Pleasure** ✳	**Play** ✳
Consistent, logical, clear reasoning, unemotional	Maintain and enhance physical well-being	Personal satisfaction, enjoyment, delight	Fun, lightness, spontaneity
Prosperity ✳	**Family** ✳	**Appearance** ✳	**Intimacy** ✳
Flourishing, well-off, affording what I want	Taking care of and spending time with loved ones	Looking good, dressing well, keeping fit	Deep emotional, spiritual connection
Aesthetic ✳	**Community** ✳	**Competence** ✠	**Achievement** ✠
Desire for beauty, artistic	Living where neighbors are close and involved	Being good at what I do, capable, effective	Successful completion of visible tasks or projects

Advancement ✠ Getting ahead, ambitious, aspiring to higher levels	**Intellectual Status** ✠ Being regarded as an expert, a person who knows	**Recognition** ✠ Getting noticed for effective efforts	**Authority** ✠ Having the power to direct events, make things happen
Power ✠ Control over other people, making them do what I want	**Competition** ✠ Winning, doing better than others	**Wild Card** _____ _____ _____	**Wild Card** _____ _____ _____
Wild Card _____ _____ _____	**Wild Card** _____ _____ _____	**Wild Card** _____ _____ _____	**Wild Card** _____ _____ _____
Wild Card _____ _____ _____	**Wild Card** _____ _____ _____	**Wild Card** _____ _____ _____	**Wild Card** _____ _____ _____